Learning to Bend

Learning to Bend

Marie Eaton

Sidekick Press
Bellingham, Washington

Publisher's Note: This is a work of creative nonfiction. While the content is based on the author's memories and personal experiences, certain names, events, and details may have been changed or reconstructed for clarity, literary effect, or to respect the privacy of individuals. Any resemblance to actual persons, living or dead, is either coincidental or used with permission.

Published 2025
Printed in the United States of America
ISBN: 978-1-958808-46-7
LCCN: 2025920021

Sidekick Press
2950 Newmarket Street, Suite 101–329
Bellingham, Washington 98226
sidekickpress.com

Learning to Bend

Cover design by Andrea Gabriel
Cover photo by Helen Scholtz

Earlier versions of two poems in this volume were previously published:

"Molting" and "Shape" appeared in *Elder Voices: Wistful, Wondering Wise* (Elder Voices Project, March 2025) as "What I Have Left Behind" and "The Body's True Shape"

"Gravity" was performed for InVerse Functions at the Infinity Box Theater Project in April 2025.

Contents

Learning to Bend

Bamboo bends in the wind,
bowing gracefully
then rising to dance again.

Light bends, traveling
from air into water, slowing
to illuminate dark depths.

River bends to wander—
a curve past tulip fields
on her way to the delta flats.

Willow bends, tossing branches
in the storm, brushing arms
against meadow grasses.

Woman bends, all stiff back
and old bones, as she learns to bow
toward an unknown future.

Homecoming
(ghazal)

Close your eyes. Listen for the melody. You may discover it again.
An elusive tune invites you to discover it again.

Daily chores and duties call. Distract. Hold all your yearning.
Desire dims, but in a single glance, you discover it again.

Guns and broken promises shatter beliefs. Faith cracks
and frays, yet in one outstretched hand, you discover it again.

Learn what fading flowers know. Bend away from growth,
and when spring arrives, you discover it again.

Close the door, begin the journey. After months of wandering,
return. Name it home as you discover it again.

Hurry

My instinct is to hurry.
There's not much time left
as sand in the hourglass
sifts down.

I pack my days
with alarmed reminders
for meetings
and appointments.

Yet, at the end of the day,
I gather in only
blurred memories,
garbled fragments of the rush.

Perhaps I should go
down to the garden
and spend an hour meditating
on snowdrops.

Free

On days when piles
of to-do tasks stand taller
than the door jamb
and will not be quiet,

when the waited-for phone call
does not come
and the mailbox holds
only advertising flyers,

when my body is weighted
by ache and gravity
and spirit becomes opaque
with despair and loss,

it is then I find myself longing
for the end of everything,
for that day when life falls away
and I am absolutely free.

Molting

Walking down this path
toward my horizon,
I find myself shedding
titles and responsibilities,

worn and full of holes,
old garments that once
served their purpose
but no longer warm me.

And my backpack, filled
with others' expectations,
I now drop in the grass
and continue with a lighter step.

Soon I will kick off my shoes,
feel the ground beneath bare feet,
and finally strip away pants and shirt
to arrive at the end, naked as I came.

Unburdened

Leave behind your extra baggage.
You won't need it for this journey.
Just gather a few things to take along.

Collect the notes your lover sent
and the clear agate stone
from the beach you walked together.

Tie together a collection
of your favorite songs and throw in
a couple of poems for good measure.

Pack up memories of walking
through wet grass in early morning
to smell the scent of purple lilacs.

Wrap everything in your red scarf,
throw the bundle over your shoulder,
and head out, on your way.

Fragrance

I walk alone through tall grass,
trailing my hands through
rosemary bushes to gather scent
on my fingertips, earthy and pungent.
They say that smell is the last memory to go.

So, when angels gather my spirit
and fly into the endless beyond,
I will drag my fingers through
lemon blossoms and rosemary needles
and carry the bouquet of this life with me.

Empty Boat

At the end of a long wharf
an empty boat waits
to carry one traveler
across black water—

faster than light,
toward the farthest edge,
propelled by spirit,
no oars needed.

All belongings left behind,
memory fragments,
and the detritus of living
scatter in piles on the dock.

Not Yet

We were young,
summer stretching out from the last day of school
toward a parade of bumpy bike rides
and dripping ice cream cones.

When our mothers called us in for chores or bedtime,
we grumbled and whined:
Not yet! Too soon!

Now, many years unwind behind us.
Clocks tick faster,
light returning leads
toward the leaving light.

When death calls us in for that final sleep,
will we still groan and wail?
Not yet. Too soon.

Cosmic Balance

On one side, a pesky angel
stacks all the tunes and melodies
of a lifetime, then places
the quiet of eternity on the other.

When I die, I hope music
tips the scale heavy,
outweighing
all that silence.

Edges

Around the edges of life,
let us gather at the boundary
of memories.

That bouquet or blanket
may calm and comfort
our anxious hearts

as we wait for the moment
on some sharp morning,
when we cross that threshold

and all edges vanish.

Traveling
(haibun)

My first step toward mortality began when I arrived, birthed,
squalling and wet, into the surprised arms of a receptionist in
the Phoenixville Hospital lobby. Along the way, I have taken
many side trips—through lemon-scented orchards, across
sunbaked red-dirt Kenyan highlands, up humid white-oak
hollows in Appalachia, and along the cool grey-blue edge of
the bay below my home.

Yet Death, I always travel toward you, comforted by the span
and textures of time, by memories gathered in sweet-scented
bundles.

> in no hurry to leave
> I wonder who might catch me
> on the other side

Echo

Clock coil unwinding,
hands race across numbered years.

Early winter winds strip the leaves,
branches bare against a pale blue sky.

Under the snow, tulips sleep
as they wait for someone else's spring.

I walk, slowly, slowly
toward that next horizon,

and somewhere it all will resolve
into a fading melody's last echo.

Time

When we were young, clocks had no meaning.
Time rolled slowly across summer grass,
through long wet days of sprinkler spray
and twilight games of kick-the-can.

In our middle years, clock hands sped faster and faster.
We changed diapers and kissed skinned knees
between classes and committee meetings,
rushing from morning coffee to bedtime collapse.

Now suddenly time unfolds,
inviting me to eat a ripe peach,
to listen to morning robins and horned owls at dusk,
whispering that she will be leaving soon.

Waiting Room

It seems we are gathered
in a crowded waiting room.
Chatting idly or playing cards,
we are immigrants waiting for an exit visa,
not sure when our names will be called.

We sit in shabby chairs, paging through
old *National Geographic* or *People* magazines
while we nibble on snack bars
and apples, waiting to be summoned.
There is only one way out of here.

In time, we will watch others leave.
Here one second, playing an ace
to take the trick—then gone
in a sudden dash through the final door,
leaving cards strewn across the table.

Others leave with tentative steps,
shedding memories and belongings.
Books and sweaters lie in heaps,
alongside small piles of tools,
empty pill bottles and vases of wilted flowers.

Some find themselves hustled through the exit,
startled surprise written on their faces.
Perhaps they expected a solo journey.
Annoyed in a crowd created by crash or calamity,
they howl: *Wait! It's not my turn yet.*

Your Plate

You might wish for filet mignon
or three bronzed scallops
nestled on a bed of lemon risotto
with a side of roasted broccolini,
but tonight's dinner is black beans and rice.

Simple. Perhaps seasoned
with a little garlic and cumin,
and in its own way, delicious.
Step back from that other longing.
Taste what's in front of you.

What Remains

All those frets and worries
you have been holding so tightly?
Open your hands and let them go,
whispers the wind.
Chant as you watch them waft away,
so much lighter than you imagined.

All that grime and nastiness
that coats your thoughts?
Slide into the stream and let them go,
murmurs the water.
Cry as they dissolve and disappear,
until all is clear, all is clean.

All those unwanted memories,
the hurts you hold in your heart?
Pile them crosswise and light a match,
sighs the fire.
Sing as you watch them smolder and flame,
until only purified ash remains.

Path

Don't ask permission.
All along, you have known what to do.

The way opens right in front of you,
waiting.

Your name is *Follow Me*—
so, start walking.

Do not stop until you know
this path well, with both your feet.

Your name is *I'll Take a Chance*.
You will, one step at a time,

and in your leaving
find your arrival.

Dark

Go out into the dusk.
Leave your flashlight
and expectations behind.

Get lost in the shadows.
Wander and wonder
with no destination in mind.

Let your feet follow a path
out under the sweep of stars
and the rising moon.

Lean your back into
cedar's rough bark
and wait.

Stand quietly in cool air
as shadows
lose their shape.

Listen to wind
whisper rumors about
the leaving light.

Open your body
to the dark
and melt into midnight.

Close your eyes and hold
night's folded flower
in your forever hands.

Credo

I believe in green,
in the push of new life
at the tips of bare branches,
the first tendrils breaking
through my garden bed.

I believe in rich brown compost
and in pink wrigglers
that turn my kitchen scraps
into the miracle
of humus and hope.

I believe in the red feather flash,
of a hawk swooping past
my writing window,
riding currents of air
over dancing cedars.

I believe in the grey-blue bay
that stretches out
toward dusky islands,
lifting my spirit out
and over the horizon.

I believe in deep purple lilacs,
myriad blossoms
broadcasting
their sweet heavy scent
as I pass.

I believe in yellow-bellied
bumblebees, nosing
into each flower's heart,
carrying secrets
of pollen and possibility.

First Sunrise

Each morning, come
to the day as if you
were the first sunrise.

Spread your radiance
across all the horizons
of your life.

Paint the soft light
of forgiveness
over yesterday's rubble.

Then, pick up a stone
and begin
to build again.

Easy to Love

It's easy to love your child when she is sleeping,
sticky fingers tucked under her pillow,
tousled curls waiting for morning's brush.
But how do you love the screaming tantrum,
the book thrown across the room,
I hate you hurled like a javelin toward your heart?

It's easy to love the endorphin high of a morning run,
to watch the sun rise over foggy hills
as lungs pull in oxygen to power pumping legs.
But how do you love the pain in arthritic knees,
your body telling you that each morning is one more toward
the day when you will have to say, *I can't run anymore?*

It's easy to love writing a poem when the words fall
lightly across the page, tumbling into couplets,
complete with scansion and alliteration.
But how do you love the blank screen, the empty mind,
the reach for words that don't arrive, except
You're no writer whispered under your breath?

Stand still
and hold the scream,
the stubborn ache,
and the emptiness
close to your heart.
You will hear what love has to say.

Meditation

Just for a moment
I can quiet the ghosts in my head.

Gossip and chatter vanish,
and silence settles in—

a mist over calm water,
an unlit candle.

Only three quiet stones
and breath after breath.

Then the bell chimes
and I put on morning's cloak,

fold the silence
into a pocket,

and wander out
into a new day.

Morning

I walk out at sunrise
into a dazzle of dawn and dew.
I lay down all my troubles,
just to hear the morning say
be here now.

Scatter all those frets and fusses
you carry in your hand.
Relinquish every should and ought
and everything you've planned—
be here now.

Light gilds the backs of far-off hills
and spreads across the bay.
Tipsy gulls swirl through the sky,
wings flashing white and grey, calling
be here now.

Shape

Perhaps this is what
growing older means.

Unraveling the snarled ball
of regrets and wonders,
hurts and healing,
strides and stumbles.

Holding each for a moment,
then dropping them into a pile
of things to forget.
Unbuckling the too-tight belt.

All weakness and worry,
boundaries and borders,
will fade away with the release
of belly and breath.

Hear the sigh of relief as body
accepts its true shape.

Ventricle

Set beating years ago,
four weeks after
sperm met egg

in my mother's womb,
this old ticker
is not reliable anymore.

Squeezing and releasing
100,000 times each year,
perhaps it's just tired.

Atrium sends messages,
electrical short circuits,
ignored by ventricle,

like a couple who,
angry with each other,
have stopped talking.

Install a pacemaker,
a therapist sent
to translate,

to poke the reluctant
ventricle as if to say,
You may be tired but answer her!

Il Pleut

Sorrow's ceaseless rain falls on
so many delicious, beautiful things:

an artichoke, a perfect persimmon,
and one ripe pear;

sunlight through cherry and redbud blossoms
amid a green drift of leaves;

new moon's sickle rising
over curving blue hills;

and echoes of a wistful Edith Piaf song,
humming in the shower.

Da Capo

In this orchestra of body and limb,
I thought I was the conductor,
waking each day to a new score.

Heart's drum setting
a steady duple rhythm,
adagio in rest, andante at morning,

and a burst of allegro
as I swerve to avoid a collision
or at the sight of my love.

Lungs (the wind section, of course)
pulling oxygen to bubble an arpeggio
through veins and arteries.

It takes so many organs,
each with its own pitch and motif,
to weave this symphony together.

Then each evening, a diminuendo—
a long rest until morning, when it's da capo,
as the orchestra tunes up to begin again.

Enough

Those younger days,
so full of yearning,
I was fretful and anxious
about tomorrow's tasks,
always peeking around
the doorframe, worried
about an unanswered
phone call, or feeling impatient
for the next guest to arrive.

These older days,
I hold a cup of mint tea
and warm my hands
as I watch birds swoop
through bare branches.
This moment
is quite enough.

Stagger

Each year carries a message
or bequest, and so memories
now pile in my arms—
first child, first steps, first words,
second marriage, many friends.

Small heartbreaks, love songs,
speeches and stages,
meetings and missteps
and losses so deep
they swallow me whole.

Years are heavy gifts to carry.
Their weight slows my steps
as I struggle up and over the next hill,
trudging toward my eighth decade,
Yet still I breathe gratitude,
and stagger from the joy of living.

Lists

I make myself lists these days.
Reminders of things to do.
Niggling thoughts that wake
me in the middle of the night.

Someone I should call.
A letter I should send.
A line for a song I am writing.
Something from the store.

I used to hold all these
in my head, rarely forgetting.
But now thoughts slide away,
leave my hands grasping air.

I used to remember
a vast catalog of lyrics.
Words effortlessly appeared,
linked boxcars down melody's track.

Phrases show up in fragments now,
hang just behind the tongue,
slide into static and mumbles.
And so, I write lists.

Shoes

My shoes don't seem to fit these days.
Like Cinderella's stepsisters,
I shoe-horn my reluctant heels in,
wedge bunions and hammer toes,
pinched and just a little angry,
under laces.

Walking is no longer the easy swing
of hip and thigh around the lake,
but a constant conversation
as metatarsal aches
call up the leg with every step.

Perhaps,
I should just buy
bigger shoes
to hold these ugly feet.

For a Tree
(tanka)

Moss, daybreak dew pearled,
in sunlit bright green patches
against your grey skin.
Tangled in feathering fronds,
tousled like morning hair.

I lay my wrinkled hand
on your lichen-covered bark.
I am growing old and wise,
but your roots run deeper,
into now and forever.

Handrail
(haibun)

No matter what you do to try to stop it, Old Age creeps up
    behind you on the stairs, waiting to give you a little shove.
    Hang on to the handrail! It lurks in nighttime shadows to
    cast a dark net over the path that used to be easy to see
    without a flashlight. It wakes you from deep sleep to empty
    an insistent bladder, and then keeps you awake, tossing on a
    rumpled pillow and listening to midnight podcasts.

Old Age pinches nerves in your hips as, step by step, you and
    your walking poles slowly climb the long hill leading you
    home. It flips pages of the calendar, faster and faster,
    scattering days and weeks across the horizon.

            I'm still here
            as sun spins through another year
            bless all my wrinkles

Solace

This is human instinct,
to go to ground when hurting,
to find a hole to hide in,

to turn our backs on the world,
lick our wounds, and trace
our scars with dirty fingernails.

Solace lies in this deeper darkness,
in the belly of the cave
where all prayers might be answered.

And someday, when all hurting ends,
buried or spread,
we go back to dark ground again.

Waiting

Sometimes at the end,
when we know death is near,
there is just the waiting.

All the rest of the world
shrinks down to this singularity—
one breath and then another.

I sit by your side,
counting seconds between
each inhalation.

I watch your skin grow pale
as sunlight travels across
the quilt on your bed.

And, although the earth still turns
on its relentless journey
around that bright star,

in this room, all time stops
as I quietly wait
for your last exhale.

Bookmark

I'm not looking for you, but there you are,
grinning up from an old photograph
tucked between the pages of a poetry book.

I can't remember why I slipped you in
between Mary Oliver's *hungry bear of death*
and John Freeman's meditation on *grief's cruelest translation.*

Perhaps I was using the photo as a bookmark
while searching for poems to read to my students
in a class on *Death and Dying* all those years ago,

back before that hungry bear took you
and cruel grief's longing for what could never be
spilled my tears upon your smiling face.

Grief

That wild animal
cannot be tamed.

She hides during the daylight
when small distractions

tug for your attention:
to-do lists, appointments,

sorting closets and drawers
into *keep* or *give away.*

But come evening, she circles—
on the hunt for tears and sorrows.

She slinks into your bedroom
to gnaw at your wounded heart.

When you know she is coming,
you open the door and invite her in.

You welcome her and count
yourself lucky to be her prey

as she feasts on all the love that now
has nowhere else to go.

Low Tide

Someday, it may happen.
You might open your eyes
to a morning that opens to tender joy.

See, there's a wide-open stretch
of beach ahead as sorrow ebbs
into the shallows for just a while.

Go ahead. Walk away from your grief
and into sunlight for a moment.
Breathe in silence and solace

and know the tide will return.

Masks

When you have nothing left to hide,
when all facades have fallen

into rubble at your scarred feet
and you stand naked in the light,

when you open your fists and heart
and offer your soul to the world,

then, a new path will open.
If you take the first step

and resist the urge to gather
shields and armor,

you may find someone
even you did not know

hidden behind those masks.

Zazen

I can sit on this mountain top,
alone and still in cool silence,
surrounded by rock and sky.
I can open my hands
and let this grief for the world
drift away on the winds.

Far below there are wars,
sound bites and shouting,
fires, floods, and famine,
but up here I can rest in clear air,
cupping a sea of mist
within the quiet holiness of snow.

The Race

No matter how fast you run,
death will always run faster.

As you round that last curve
heading for the finish line,

she will catch up
and take your hand.

You will break the tape,
running together.

What Matters

Receipts murmur on my desk,
reminding me it's tax time.

Laundry in the basket clamors
to be folded, hung, put away.

Emails litter my in-box, mutter
and demand my attention.

Voice messages and missed calls
beg for me to join, attend, respond.

For today, I will ignore them,
peel away disruptions,

diversions and distractions,
to find the heart of what matters:

breath to fill my lungs,
a song to soothe my soul.

Thread

You may be distracted
by something that glitters
just out of sight,
be thrown off course
by side winds.

You may pause
when the cougar hidden
in dark trees along the path
flickers into sight
and growls low.

But if hand over hand
you follow the true thread,
you will find your destination
and in arriving
discover your beginning.

Begin

Through an open window,
tanagers and meadowlarks
call down the day
opening into dawn.

Morning unfurls
across grass and bloom,
as night's dark origami
unfolds into daylight.

Window

The imperfect stitch,
a planned flaw
in this prayer rug

left by the maker,
acknowledges that only Allah
can create perfection.

Such intentional imperfection,
subtle and sly,
perhaps a different color wool

on one flower petal,
cracks open a window
for the prayer to leave,

to do its perfect work
in an imperfect world.

Hibernate

When the days shorten
and the world darkens
as Earth spins on her axis,
everything slows down.

The simplest task
takes forever.
Feet drag through
dim afternoon light.

Even trees are quiet.
Softly falling rain
slides through bare branches,
puddles at their feet.

Birds who stayed
skip their morning song
to huddle in nests,
heads tucked under wings.

Perhaps like the bear
we should hibernate,
sleep away winter doldrums
to awaken in spring,

ravenous for light.

Questions

What is tucked in the bark of the old oak
at the bottom of the garden
as leaves turn golden in fall's cool air?

Nestled inside the tomato seed,
pushed into deep, dark spring dirt
as soft rains drench the garden path?

Lurking at the threshold of a baby's laugh,
pealing like ringing bells
across the smell of summer roses?

Slipped into the bluest egg,
protected in dark warmth
under the robin's wing?

Sheltered in salmon roe,
glistening at river bottom,
waiting to turn again to life?

When answers fall
into your open heart,
a thousand silent bells will ring.

Wish

I wish I could lie
on warm beach sand,
spread out like seaweed strands,
wait for the sea to return
from the low tide
to slowly lift me.

I wish I could lift
my arms out wide,
stretch them like wings,
wait for the wind to return
from the other side of clouds
to slowly carry me away.

I wish I could drop
my imagined paths
of ought and obligation,
want and will,
to find where water
and wind might take me.

Shimmer

Shuffle through your stack of days.
Find one that shimmers.

Haul her out and set her on her feet
to walk around a bit,

wobbly at first, dressed in tattered
remnants of recollection.

As she begins to reminisce,
walk together down memory's path,

stoop to turn over stones and reveal
details you thought forgotten:

The bitter taste of oranges in Valencia.
A subway saxophone's wail.

Blueberries eaten slowly, one by one,
under a pale Munich morning sky.

Sweat on your skin as you danced
in the Nyiri Desert under the Milky Way.

You Think You Know

When something you think you know
sails across the sky,

when birds in formation point
toward a southern skyline,

when cloud ships coast on the wind
in a whirl of rusty autumn leaves,

or a singing moon crosses the horizon—
let yourself wonder if perhaps

angels stride across the heavens.

Liminal
(duplex)

On foggy fall mornings in that liminal space
between sky and sea, I have questions.

        Questions fold between sky and sea,
        yet I have not found answers.

Once I thought I knew answers,
then life toppled all I believed about sea and sky,

        spilling every certainty and belief,
        shattered on doubt's dusty floor.

You knelt beside me on that dusty floor,
gathered up shards of my broken spirit.

        Gently collected these fragments and shards
        till sadness and doubt turned into joy.

So joyfully I turn to look for you
on foggy fall mornings in that liminal space.

Gravity

I've seen film clips of astronauts
floating weightless in spaceships,
revolving head over heels,
spinning and looping, arms akimbo.

Some seek that thrill,
running headlong down ski slopes,
in roller coasters or bungee jumping,
a weightless moment of letting go.

I prefer when gravity's hand
holds me close so I know
exactly where is up
and where I will land

when like Newton's apple
I finally fall.

A World Apart

Crimson and orange bands of light
layer across the backs of blue islands in the bay
as evening leans on the deck rail in my quiet town.

In my neighborhood, kids leave scraps
of hamburger and potato fries strewn
across dinner tables as they run out to play.

Halfway across the globe,
rocket trails blaze crimson and orange
through rubbled dust clouds over the city.

On that other street, children gaze
quiet and hollow-eyed as they eat
scraps of bread or a rotting apple.

Here, mothers tuck their children
into warm beds, read *Goodnight Moon*,
and plant a kiss on sleepy heads.

There, mothers write on their children's arms
so that when bombs fall and buildings collapse,
someone will know their names.

Candle
(golden shovel)

Some moments are flame.
There was a time
I wanted a promise
we would not burn.
　　　　　　—Rosemerry Wahtola Trommer

We knelt in the dark to ask for some
relief from mounting moments
of despair about our nation that are
fanning the flame
of angst and anxiety. We paused there
hoping that the unease that was
spinning through a
telescoping tunnel of time
might melt away. I
knew we wanted
an answer, a
savior, but holding prayers and a promise,
we bowed our heads until we
understood that nothing outside would
save us. Not
one unlit candle would burn.

Blue

Daylight stretches between sunrise and sunset,
draped across rolling blue hills,
gilding newly green fir needle bundles.

Birds flicker in and out of sight,
casting reflections on slate grey water,
stitching clouds to a pale azure sky.

Blue hydrangeas wave pom-poms
in the wind. Blueberries hang in heavy clusters,
ready for the white bowl.

On the radio, a woman belts out Chicago blues,
her chocolate voice riding high
on a saxophone's wail.

The day has much to do before
indigo evening arrives, inviting night to
unbutton the stars and set the moon to sail.

Last Dance

Death offers her hand
and invites you to begin
the infinite dance.

Her feet move in ceaseless rhythms.
She knows how to lead,
so take her hand.

Bend to her insistent melody,
captured inside black vinyl grooves,
where her universe twirls and turns.

You don't know these steps,
but back before time began,
she took tango lessons.

Lean into her shoulder
and accept the beginning
of everything.

Miracles

When the curtain of ordinary rises
from the daily grind and drudge,

there is a miraculous
shining world within a world.

Sweet cream butter melts on
a loaf of bread, warm from the oven.

Kelp, pulled by tides from deep waters,
piles on a beach as terns wheel above.

Dusky white flowers bloom
on the gnarled pear tree.

Stars slip through night's hand
to shimmer and fall.

We lay silver Milagro charms on an altar,
our prayers for a cure.

Gasp

In the miracle of my garden,
a wee green frog perches
on top of the pump handle.

Until I see it, everything is ordinary:
Just weeds and dirt
and a row to hoe.

Suddenly, all is wondrous:
Luminous skin, webbed toes,
his eyes staring into mine.

We both
hold
our breath.

Break

On a day like today,
when blue skies and the open bay
call outside my window,
I lay down my chores
and walk out into
the summer morning.

I leave behind dancing dust
and a pile of unfolded sheets
singing in the laundry basket.
As I close the door behind me,
I can hear unwashed dishes
gossiping about my housekeeping.

I wander out, dragging my hands
through fragrant rosemary and oregano,
past bee-humming heather
into deep awnings of greening trees,
and vow not to return until
the sun's red lip kisses the horizon.

Astonishment

When dawn lifts her grey wing
to reveal tender pink feathers,

I want to lay down
lists, tasks and duties,

and turn toward wonder—
to write poems, to make love.

Between

I don't know if January is male or female,
or something in between.

In the morning, *she* wraps herself in a pale grey shawl
and sits quietly looking through the window,

but by evening *he* sends the garbage can lid
spinning down the driveway in a gusty fit of wind.

In some languages, all words are gendered,
every object assigned as masculine or feminine,

and each word spoken shapes
our understanding of the roles we must play.

The feminine spoon or cup.
The manly hammer.

But my hands want to hold both
as I stand balanced somewhere in between.

Inside Me

(with a nod to Walt Whitman's "Song of Myself")

Inside me are multitudes.

An angry adolescent
who won't take no for an answer,
who strides across the room
to argue with that whole congregation
down on their knees,
sending up prayers for salvation from sin.

A crone, rising late
from morning's cloudy bed,
bemoaning the ache and creak
of every ancient bone,
every inch of slack skin, the taste
of age bitter in her mouth.

A bossy midwife
who shouts *keep pushing*
as inspiration turns into labor,
and she coaxes the miracle of each
new song or poem
onto the page.

A gentle griever, cradling
an aching heart in her hands,
as she wades through seas of tears
to seek an offered cup
of solace and consolation
and a quiet place to lie down.

A harried housekeeper,
washing sheets and secretly wishing
as she folds the laundry
that she could join a choir of angels
singing old pop songs
in ethereal four-part harmony.

Vigilance

I listen to the news.
Be on the watch, they say.

I hear the warnings,
count my change and lock my door.

On guard for scam emails
flooding my inbox,

I keep an eye out
for the driver with road rage,

the man in a hoodie behind me,
boots slapping the pavement.

But I would rather be on the watch
for a heron lifting from the pond,

a red leaf spinning down the path,
the Snow Moon rising behind eastern hills,

and a kind stranger stooping to pick up
the package I dropped in the post office line.

This is surveillance to feed the soul.

You

I have known you
like blackberry knows sun,
tomato knows vine,

frog knows pond and lily leaf,
hummingbird knows blossom,

eagle knows wind,
and salmon knows river.

Our way today recalls
familiar yesterdays.

I know you the way my heart
longing for melody
finds music.

Gifts

I came bringing bunches of lilacs
to lay at your door,

a poem tucked into their fragrant
blooming purple.

I came carrying ripe red cherries
in my open hands.

You opened the door, read the poem,
smelled the blossoms, ate a cherry,

and smiled. And then
you gave me everything.

Pomegranate

Break open a pomegranate. Let each bright red aril
glisten in the light. Thread your thumb along the ribs.

Push deep into the fruit. Each cleft and crevice
holds a craving for taste and touch.

Gently release these nubs of yearning
until each kernel falls softly into your palm.

Let your lips kiss the blush of bright nectar
on your fingers as you sip and swallow

until, with a quick nip, the berry
of liquid love breaks open.

Arrows

Hands clapping,
the congregation raises voices
in a rock and roll of gratitude.
Bodies sway in celebration.

Songs of radiant praise swell,
spreading joy. Each heart sings
with fiery explosions of love
as worship pours light into the world.

These hymns mean business.
Arrows—fletched with electric organ lutes
and pointing toward heaven—
aim straight at God's heart.

New Year's Eve

Another year rides in on quiet snow.
White drifts and mounds cover everything.

As light moves from east to west,
the planet swings once more around our star.

Tonight, we will turn a calendar page
and close doors that will never open again.

I vow to fold my resolutions into paper cranes
and, unburdened, welcome the new year

as I burn them all in a cleansing fire.

.

Devotion

I approach
each day
as an offering
from a kind spirit.

Rising at dawn,
I wander through darkness
until sun paints
roses across my wall.

I carry this memory
through the arc of day
in a pocket
just over my heart.

At evening's edge,
I take it out again
and send it back
to the wind.

Notes on Poems and Poetic Forms

Page 38, "Bookmark"
I taught a course on Death and Dying at Fairhaven College, Western Washington University. The poems referenced here are Mary Oliver's "When Death Comes" from *Devotions: The Selected Poems of Mary Oliver* (Penguin Press, an imprint of Penguin Random House LLC, 2017) and John Freeman's "Saudade" (https://pickmeuppoetry.org/saudade-by-john-freeman).

Page 2, "Homecoming"
A *ghazal* is a poetic form originating in Arabic literature. It consists of a series of couplets, each expressing a complete thought, that share a rhyme scheme and refrain.

Pages 12 and 35, "Traveling" and "Handrail"
A *haibun* is a Japanese literary form that combines prose with haiku.

Page 53, "Liminal"
A duplex poem arranges fourteen lines in couplets. The second line of the first couplet is echoed in the first line of the second couplet, and this pattern continues until the last line, which echoes the first.

Page 56, "Candle"

In the golden shovel form, the ending words of each line collectively read as an excerpt from another poem. This poem uses the first four lines of Rosemerry Wahtola Trommer's "No Regret" from *All the Honey* (Samara Press, 2023). Used with permission of the author.

Acknowledgments

My gratitude to Helen Scholtz for sharing the lovely cover photograph.

Thank you to Susan Bond, whose gentle suggestions and careful copyediting helped polish these poems.

I am indebted to my early morning writing group, who faithfully show up on Zoom six days a week to open space for our shared creativity, offering prompts that sparked many of these poems, and thanks also to the Thursday Poets, Eileen, Clare, and Linda, whose feedback has honed my writing skills.

And, acknowledging that artists and writers can best flourish with the loving support of others, I again say thank you to my wife, Mary Ellen, for always making room in our long-intertwined lives for me to do this creative work.